PIANO • VOCAL • GUITAR

MORE SONGS OF THE NINETIES

THE DECADE SERIES

D1305846

ISBN 0-7935-9802-8

HAL•LEONARD®
CORPORATION
7777 W. BLUEMOUND RD. P.O. BOX 13819 MILWAUKEE, WI 53213

Visit Hal Leonard Online at
www.halleonard.com

MORE SONGS OF THE NINETIES

THE DECADE SERIES

Contents

ALL BY MYSELF

Music by SERGEI RACHMANINOFF
Words and Additional Music by ERIC CARMEN

When I was young, — I nev - er

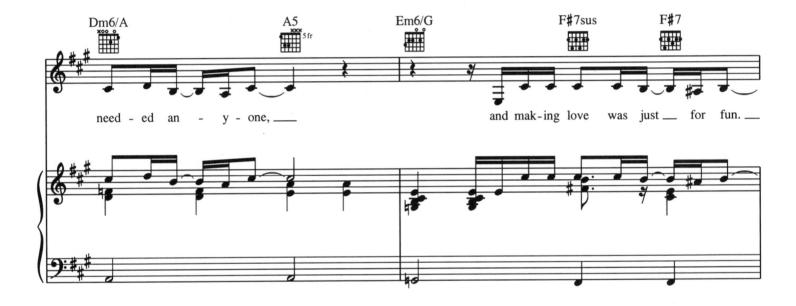

need - ed an - y - one, ___ and mak-ing love was just ___ for fun.

Those days ___ are gone. ___

ALL MY LIFE

Words by JOEL HAILEY
Music by JOEL HAILEY and RORY BENNETT

Original key: D♭ major. This edition has been transposed down one half-step to be more playable.

ALWAYS BE MY BABY

Words and Music by MARIAH CAREY,
JERMAINE DUPRI and MANUEL SEAL

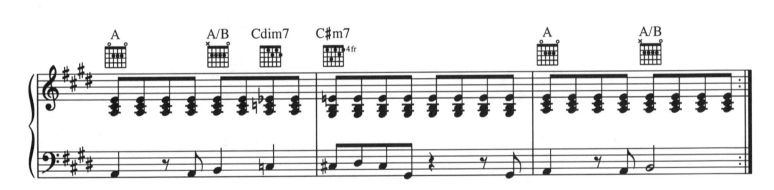

We were as one, _ babe   for a mo-ment in ____ time. _
I ain't gon-na cry, _ no,   and I won't beg you to ____ stay. _

Boy, don't you know you can't es-cape_ me. Ooh dar-ling, cause you'll al - ways be _ my ba -

- by. And we'll lin - ger on. ___ Time can't e-rase a feel-ing this strong. ___

No way you're ev - er gon - na shake_ me. Ooh dar-ling, 'cause you'll al - ways be _ my ba -

- by. ___

BUILDING A MYSTERY

Words and Music by SARAH McLACHLAN
and PIERRE MARCHAND

BLUE

Words and Music by
BILL MACK

BUTTERFLY KISSES

Words and Music by RANDY THOMAS
and BOB CARLISLE

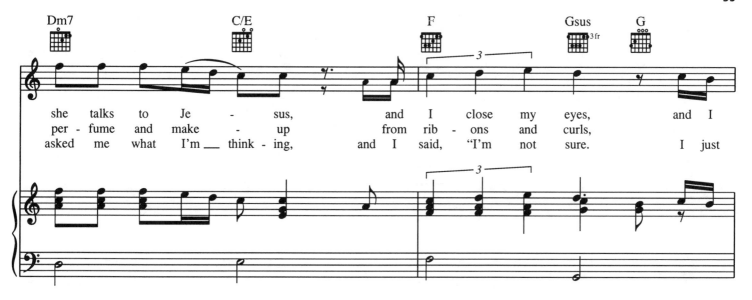

she talks to Je - sus, and I close my eyes, and I
per - fume and make - up from rib - ons and curls,
asked me what I'm ___ think - ing, and I said, "I'm not sure. I just

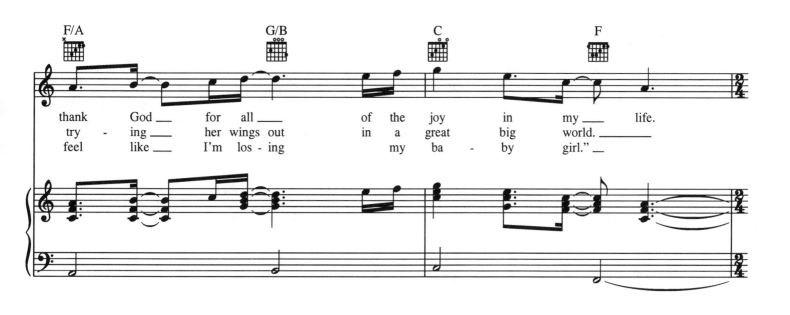

thank God ___ for all ___ of the joy in my ___ life.
try - ing ___ her wings out in a great big world. _____
feel like ___ I'm los - ing my ba - by girl." ___

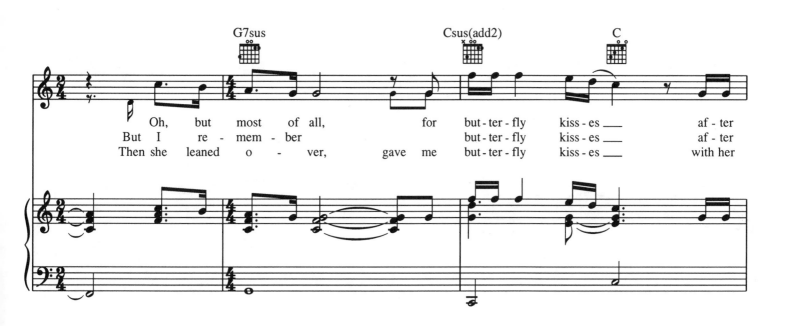

Oh, but most of all, for but - ter - fly kiss - es ___ af - ter
But I re - mem - ber but - ter - fly kiss - es ___ af - ter
Then she leaned o - ver, gave me but - ter - fly kiss - es ___ with her

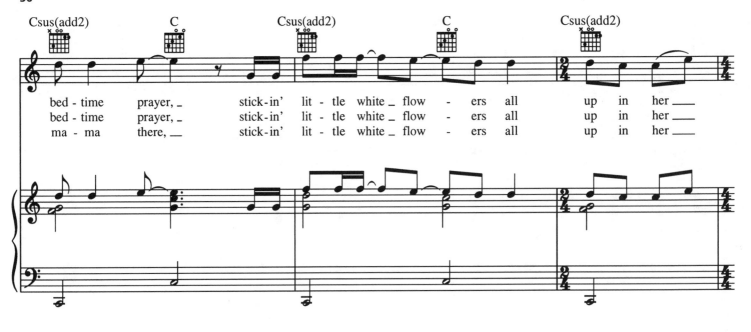

bed - time prayer, _ stick-in' lit - tle white _ flow - ers all up in her ___
bed - time prayer, _ stick-in' lit - tle white _ flow - ers all up in her ___
ma - ma there, ___ stick-in' lit - tle white _ flow - ers all up in her ___

hair. "Walk be - side ___ the po - ny, dad - dy, it's
hair. "You know how much _ I love _ you, dad - dy, but if
hair. "Walk me down _ the aisle, _ dad - dy, it's

my first ride. ___ I know the cake _ looks fun - ny, dad - dy, but
you don't mind, ___ I'm on - ly goin' _ to kiss _ you on ___ the
just a - bout time. Does my wed - ding gown _ look pret - ty, dad - dy? Dad-

CAN'T HELP FALLING IN LOVE

from SLIVER

Words and Music by GEORGE DAVID WEISS,
HUGO PERETTI and LUIGI CREATORE

CANDLE IN THE WIND 1997

Music by ELTON JOHN
Words by BERNIE TAUPIN

Good-bye, Eng-land's rose; _____ may you ev - er
Love - li - ness _____ we've lost; _____ these emp - ty days

grow in our hearts. _____ You were the grace that placed it - self _____ where
with - out _____ your smile. _____ This torch we'll al - ways car - ry for our

lives were torn a - part. _____ You called out to our coun - try,
na - tion's gold - en child. _____ And e - ven though we try,

CHANGE THE WORLD
featured on the Motion Picture Soundtrack PHENOMENON

Words and Music by GORDON KENNEDY,
TOMMY SIMS and WAYNE KIRKPATRICK

If I can reach the __ stars, __
If I could be __ king, __

pull __ one down for you, __
e - ven for a day, __

CIRCLE OF LIFE
(as performed by ELTON JOHN)

Music by ELTON JOHN
Lyrics by TIM RICE

DON'T SPEAK

Words and Music by ERIC STEFANI
and GWEN STEFANI

62

EXHALE
(Shoop Shoop)
from the Original Soundtrack Album WAITING TO EXHALE

Words and Music by
BABYFACE

Easy R&B ballad

1. Ev - 'ry - one falls in love some - times. ___ Some-times it's
2.,3. laugh, some-times you'll cry. ___ Life nev - er

wrong ___ and some - times it's right. For ev - 'ry
tells __ us ___ the whens or whys. When you've got

win some - one must fail, but there comes a
friends to wish you well, you'll find a

GIVE ME ONE REASON

Words and Music by
TRACY CHAPMAN

Tune guitar down one half step.

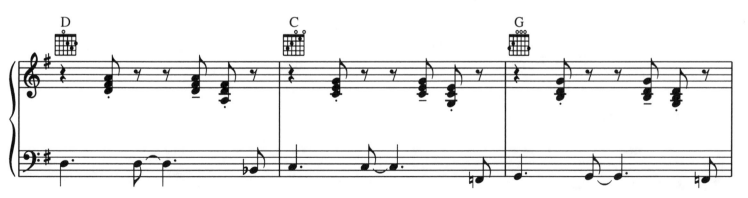

70

GO THE DISTANCE
(as performed by MICHAEL BOLTON)

Music by ALAN MENKEN
Lyrics by DAVID ZIPPEL

Have You Ever Really Loved A Woman?

from the Motion Picture DON JUAN DeMARCO

Words and Music by BRYAN ADAMS,
MICHAEL KAMEN and ROBERT JOHN LANGE

Additional Lyrics

2. To really love a woman, let her hold you
   Till ya know how she needs to be touched.
   You've gotta breathe her, really taste her.
   Till you can feel her in your blood.
   N' when you can see your unborn children in her eyes.
   Ya know ya really love a woman.

   When you love a woman
   You tell her that she's really wanted.
   When you love a woman
   You tell her that she's the one.
   Cuz she needs somebody to tell her
   That you'll always be together
   So tell me have you ever really,
   Really really ever loved a woman.

3. Instrumental

   Then when you find yourself
   Lyin' helpless in her arms.
   You know you really love a woman.

   When you love a woman *etc.*

HARD TO SAY I'M SORRY

Words and Music by PETER CETERA
and DAVID FOSTER

I CAN LOVE YOU LIKE THAT

Words and Music by STEVE DIAMOND,
MARIBETH DERRY and JENNIFER KIMBALL

I FINALLY FOUND SOMEONE

from THE MIRROR HAS TWO FACES

Words and Music by BARBRA STREISAND, MARVIN HAMLISCH,
R. J. LANGE and BRYAN ADAMS

Male: I fi-n'lly found some-one who knocks me off my feet.

I fi-n'lly found the one ___ that makes me feel com-plete.

Female: It start-ed o-ver cof-fee. We start-ed out as friends.

I DON'T WANT TO WAIT

Words and Music by
PAULA COLE

So o-pen up your morn-ing light and say a lit-tle prayer for I. You know that if we are to stay a-live, then see the peace in ev-'ry eye. Du du du du du du,

I SAY A LITTLE PRAYER

featured in the Tri-Star Motion Picture MY BEST FRIEND'S WEDDING

Lyric by HAL DAVID
Music by BURT BACHARACH

IT'S ALL COMING BACK TO ME NOW

Words and Music by
JIM STEINMAN

I'LL BE MISSING YOU

Written and Composed by
STING

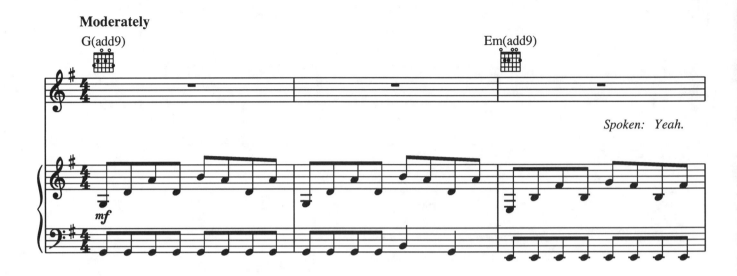

Spoken: Yeah.

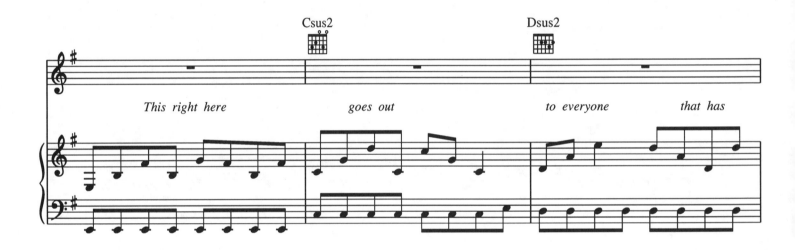

This right here   *goes out*   *to everyone*   *that has*

lost someone   *that they*   *truly love. Check it out.*

Rap 1:
Rap 2:
Rap 3:   *(See rap lyrics)*
Rap 4:

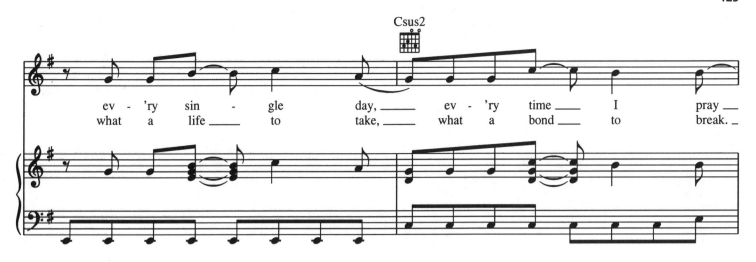

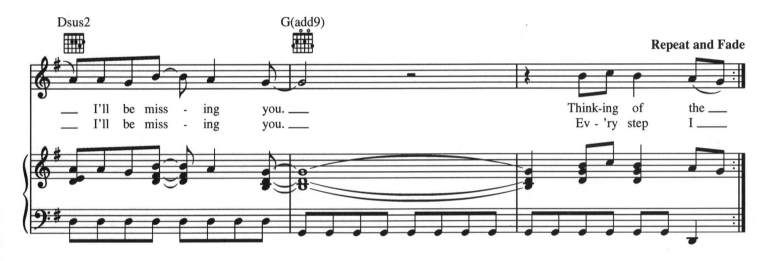

Rap Lyrics

Rap 1: Seems like yesterday we used to rock the show.
I laced the track, you locked the flow.
So far from hangin' on the block for dough.
Notorious, they got to know that life ain't always what it
Seemed to be. Words can't express what you mean to me.
Even though you're gone, we still a team.
Through your family, I'll fulfill your dreams.

Rap 2: In the future, can't wait to see if you open up the gates for me.
Reminisce sometime the night they took my friend.
Try to black it out, but it plays again.
When it's real, feelin's hard to conceal.
Can't imagine all the pain I feel.
Give anything to hear half your breath.
I know you're still livin' your life after death.

Rap 3: It's kinda hard with you not around. Know you're in heaven smilin' down
Watchin' us while we pray for you.
Ev'ry day we pray for you.
Till the day we meet again, in my heart is where I keep you, friend.
Memories give me the strength I need to proceed,
Strength I need to believe.

Rap 4: My thoughts, Big, I just can't define.
Wish I could turn back the hands of time,
Us and a six, shop for new clothes and kicks,
You and me take in flicks.
Make a hit, stages they receive you on.
Still can't believe you're gone.
Give anything to hear half your breath.
I know you're still livin' your life after death.

IT'S YOUR LOVE

Words and Music by
STEPHONY E. SMITH

Moderately

Male: Danc-in' in the dark, _____ mid-dle of the night. Tak-in' your heart _____ and hold-in' it tight. _____ E - mo-tion - al touch

THEME FROM "JURASSIC PARK"

from the Universal Motion Picture JURASSIC PARK

Composed by
JOHN WILLIAMS

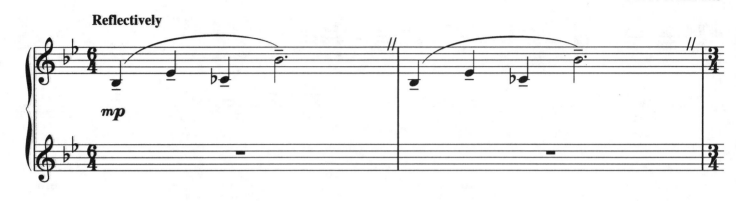

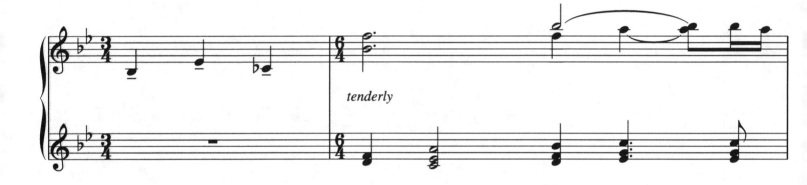

THE KEEPER OF THE STARS

Words and Music by KAREN STALEY,
DANNY MAYO and DICKEY LEE

THE LORD OF THE DANCE

By RONAN HARDIMAN

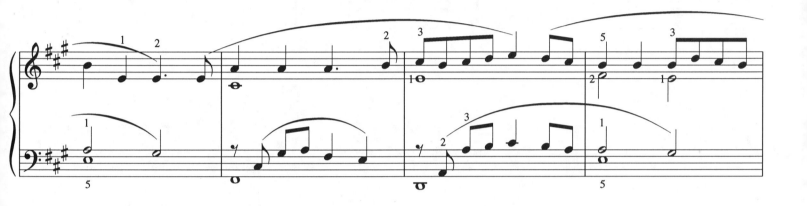

142

With spirit

LOVE OF MY LIFE

Words and Music by KEITH STEGALL
and DAN HILL

LULLABYE
(GOODNIGHT, MY ANGEL)

Words and Music by
BILLY JOEL

Good-night, my an-gel, time to close your eyes,
Good-night, my an-gel, now it's time to sleep,

and save these ques-tions for an-oth-er day.
and still so man-y things I want to say.

I think I know what you've been ask-ing me.
Re-mem-ber all the songs you sang for me

I think you know what I've been
when we went sail-ing on an

Good-night, my an - gel, now it's time to dream, and dream how won-der-ful your

life will be. Some - day your child may cry, and if you sing this lull - a - bye,

MISSION: IMPOSSIBLE THEME

from the Paramount Motion Picture MISSION: IMPOSSIBLE

By LALO SCHIFRIN

Moderately, with drive

MY ALL

Words by MARIAH CAREY
Music by MARIAH CAREY
and WALTER AFANASIEFF

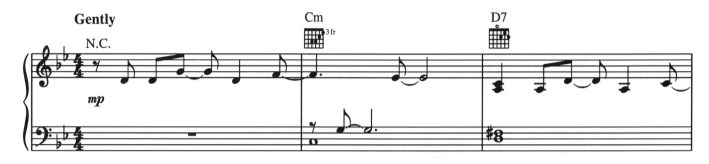

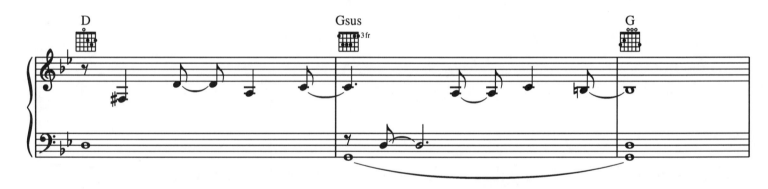

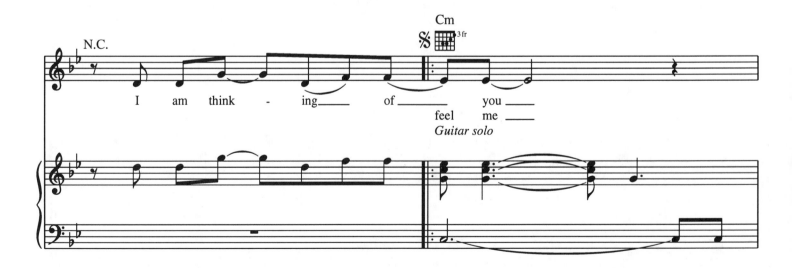

I am think - ing_ of_ you_
feel me _
Guitar solo

WHEN YOU SAY NOTHING AT ALL

Words and Music by DON SCHLITZ
and PAUL OVERSTREET

It's a-maz - ing how__ you can speak right __ to my heart.__
All day long ____ I can hear peo- ple talk - ing out loud, __

With-out say - ing a word __
but when you _ hold me near _

D.S. al Coda

The

CODA

when you say noth-ing at all. ____

rit.

MY FATHER'S EYES

Words and Music by
ERIC CLAPTON

MY HEART WILL GO ON
(Love Theme from 'Titanic')
from the Paramount and Twentieth Century Fox Motion Picture TITANIC

Music by JAMES HORNER
Lyric by WILL JENNINGS

Moderately

Ev - 'ry night in my dreams I see you, I feel you, that is how I know you go on.

VALENTINE

Words and Music by JACK KUGELL
and JIM BRICKMAN

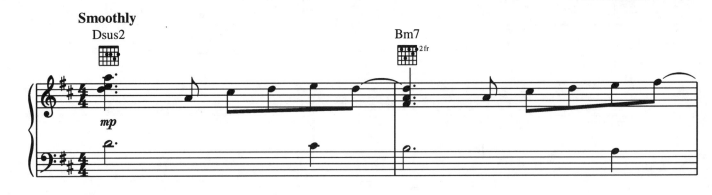

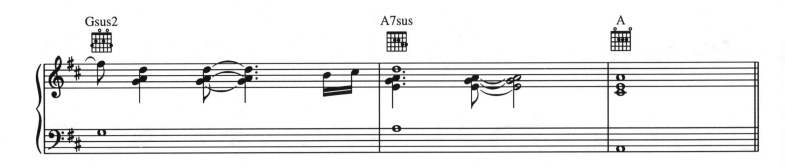

If there were no words, _ no way to speak, _ I _
All of my life, _ I have been wait - ing for _ all

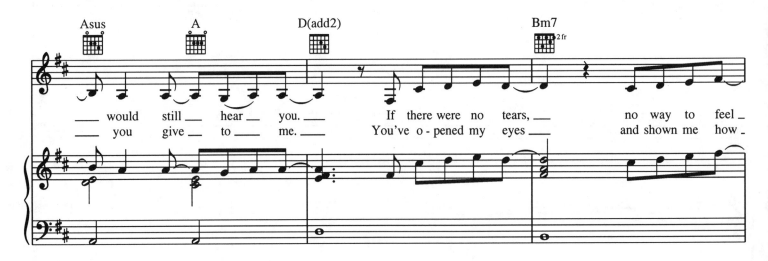

_ would still _ hear _ you. _ If there were no tears, _ no way to feel
_ you give _ to _ me. _ You've o - pened my eyes _ and shown me how

A WINK AND A SMILE

Words and Music by MARC SHAIMAN
and RAMSEY McLEAN

1. I re-mem-ber the days ___ of just keep-ing time, ___ of
2. (Instrumental solo ad lib...

hang-ing a-round ___ in ___ sleep-y towns ___ for-ev - er; ___ ...end solo)

back roads emp-ty for miles. ___
Give me a wink and a smile. ___

Well, you
(continue solo...

YOU MUST LOVE ME

from the Cinergi Motion Picture EVITA

Words by TIM RICE
Music by ANDREW LLOYD WEBBER

Additional Lyrics

Verse 2: *(Instrumental 8 bars)*
Why are you at my side?
How can I be any use to you now?
Give me a chance and I'll let you see how
Nothing has changed.
Deep in my heart I'm concealing
Things that I'm longing to say,
Scared to confess what I'm feeling
Frightened you'll slip away,
You must love me.

YOU WERE MEANT FOR ME

Words and Music by JEWEL KILCHER
and STEVE POLTZ

THE DECADE SERIES

The Decade Series explores the music of the 1890s to the 1980s through each era's major events and personalities. Each volume features text and photos and over 40 of the decade's top songs, showing how music has acted as a mirror or a catalyst for current events and trends. All books are arranged for piano, voice and guitar.

Songs Of The 1890's
55 songs, including: Asleep In The Deep • Hello! Ma Baby • Maple Leaf Rag • My Wild Irish Rose • 'O Sole Mio • The Sidewalks Of New York • Stars And Stripes Forever • Ta Ra Ra Boom De Ay • When You Were Sweet Sixteen • and more.
00311655 ....$12.95

Songs Of The 1900's – 1900-1909
57 favorites, including: By The Light Of The Silvery Moon • Fascination • Give My Regards To Broadway • Glow Worm • Meet Me In St. Louis • Take Me Out To The Ball Game • Yankee Doodle Boy • and more.
00311656 ....$12.95

Songs Of The 1910's
57 classics, including: After You've Gone • Ah! Sweet Mystery Of Life • Danny Boy • Let Me Call You Sweetheart • My Melancholy Baby • Oh, You Beautiful Doll • When Irish Eyes Are Smiling • You Made Me Love You (I Didn't Want To Do It) • and more.
00311657 ....$12.95

Songs Of The 20's
58 songs, featuring: Ain't Misbehavin' • April Showers • Baby Face • California Here I Come • Five Foot Two, Eyes Of Blue • I Can't Give You Anything But Love • Manhattan • Stardust • The Varsity Drag • Who's Sorry Now.
00361122 ....$14.95

Songs Of The 30's
61 songs, featuring: All Of Me • The Continental • I Can't Get Started • I'm Getting Sentimental Over You • In The Mood • The Lady Is A Tramp • Love Letters In The Sand • My Funny Valentine • Smoke Gets In Your Eyes • What A Diff'rence A Day Made.
00361123 ....$14.95

Songs Of The 40's
61 songs, featuring: God Bless The Child • How High The Moon • The Last Time I Saw Paris • Moonlight In Vermont • A Nightingale Sang In Berkeley Square • A String Of Pearls • Swinging On A Star • Tuxedo Junction • You'll Never Walk Alone.
00361124 ....$14.95

Songs Of The 50's
59 songs, featuring: Blue Suede Shoes • Blue Velvet • Here's That Rainy Day • Love Me Tender • Misty • Rock Around The Clock • Satin Doll • Tammy • Three Coins In The Fountain • Young At Heart.
00361125 ....$14.95

Songs Of The 60's
60 songs, featuring: By The Time I Get To Phoenix • California Dreamin' • Can't Help Falling In Love • Downtown • Green Green Grass Of Home • Happy Together • I Want To Hold Your Hand • Love Is Blue • More • Strangers In The Night.
00361126 ....$14.95

Songs Of The 70's
More than 45 songs including: Don't Cry For Me Argentina • Feelings • The First Time Ever I Saw Your Face • How Deep Is Your Love • Imagine • Let It Be • Me And Bobby McGee • Piano Man • Send In The Clowns • You Don't Bring Me Flowers • You Needed Me.
00361127 ....$14.95

Songs Of The 80's
Over 40 of this decade's biggest hits, including: Candle In The Wind • Don't Worry, Be Happy • Ebony And Ivory • Endless Love • Every Breath You Take • Flashdance...What A Feeling • Islands In The Stream • Kokomo • Memory • Sailing • Somewhere Out There • We Built This City • What's Love Got To Do With It • With Or Without You.
00490275 ....$14.95

MORE SONGS OF THE DECADE SERIES

Due to popular demand, we are pleased to present these new collections with even more great songs from the 1920s through 1980s. Each book features beautiful piano/vocal/guitar arrangements. Perfect for practicing musicians, educators, collectors, and music hobbyists.

More Songs Of The 20's
Over 50 songs, including: Ain't We Got Fun? • Bill • Carolina In The Morning • Fascinating Rhythm • The Hawaiian Wedding Song • Malagueña • Nobody Knows You When You're Down And Out • Someone To Watch Over Me • Yes, Sir, That's My Baby • and more.
00311647 ....$14.95

More Songs of the 30's
Over 50 songs, including: All The Things You Are • A Fine Romance • In A Sentimental Mood • Just A Gigolo • Let's Call The Whole Thing Off • Mad Dogs And Englishmen • Stompin' At The Savoy • Stormy Weather • Thanks For The Memory • and more.
00311648 ....$14.95

More Songs Of The 40's
Over 60 songs, including: Bali Ha'i • Be Careful, It's My Heart • Five Guys Named Moe • The Last Time I Saw Paris • Old Devil Moon • San Antonio Rose • Some Enchanted Evening • Too Darn Hot • and more.
00311649 ....$14.95

More Songs Of The 50's
56 songs, including: Blueberry Hill • Chanson D'Amour • Charlie Brown • Do-Re-Mi • Hey, Good Lookin' • Hound Dog • I Could Have Danced All Night • Mack The Knife • Mona Lisa • My Favorite Things • (Let Me Be Your) Teddy Bear • That's Amore • and more.
00311650 ....$14.95

More Songs Of The 60's
66 songs, including: Alfie • Baby Elephant Walk • Bonanza • Born To Be Wild • Eleanor Rigby • Moon River • Raindrops Keep Fallin' On My Head • Seasons In The Sun • Sweet Caroline • Tell Laura I Love Her • What The World Needs Now • Wooly Bully • and more.
00311651 ....$14.95

More Songs Of The 70's
Over 50 songs, including: Afternoon Delight • All By Myself • American Pie • Billy, Don't Be A Hero • Happy Days • Honesty • I Shot The Sheriff • Maggie May • Maybe I'm Amazed • She Believes In Me • She's Always A Woman • Wishing You Were Here • and more.
00311652 ....$14.95

More Songs Of The 80's
43 songs, including: Addicted To Love • Call Me • Don't Know Much • Footloose • Girls Just Want To Have Fun • The Heat Is On • Karma Chameleon • Longer • Straight Up • Take My Breath Away • Tell Her About It • We're In This Love Together • and more.
00311653 ....$14.95

STILL MORE SONGS OF THE DECADE SERIES

What could be better than even *more* songs from your favorite decade! These books feature piano/vocal/guitar arrangements with no duplication with *earlier volumes*.

Still More Songs Of The 30's
Over 50 songs including: April in Paris • Body And Soul • Heat Wave • It Don't Mean A Thing (If It Ain't Got That Swing) • and more.
00310027 ....$14.95

Still More Songs Of The 40's
Over 50 songs including: Any Place I Hang My Hat • Don't Get Around Much Anymore • If I Loved You • Sentimental Journey • and more.
00310028 ....$14.95

Still More Songs Of The 50's
Over 50 songs including: Autumn Leaves • Chantilly Lace • If I Were A Bell • Luck Be A Lady • The Man That Got Away • Venus • and more.
00310029 ....$14.95

Still More Songs Of The 60's
Over 50 more songs, including: Do You Know The Way To San Jose • Duke Of Earl • Hey Jude • I'm Henry VIII, I Am • Leader Of The Pack • (You Make Me Feel) Like A Natural Woman • What A Wonderful World • and more.
00311680 ....$14.95

Still More Songs Of The 70's
Over 60 hits, including: Cat's In The Cradle • Nadia's Theme • Philadelphia Freedom • The Way We Were • You've Got A Friend • and more.
00311683 ....$14.95

Contemporary Classics

Your favorite songs for piano, voice and guitar.

The Definitive Rock 'n' Roll Collection
A classic collection of the best songs from the early rock 'n' roll years – 1955-1966. 97 songs, including: Barbara Ann • Chantilly Lace • Dream Lover • Duke Of Earl • Earth Angel • Great Balls Of Fire • Louie, Louie • Rock Around The Clock • Ruby Baby • Runaway • (Seven Little Girls) Sitting In The Back Seat • Stay • Surfin' U.S.A. • Wild Thing • Woolly Bully • and more.
00490195 ....$27.95

The Big Book Of Rock
78 of rock's biggest hits, including: Addicted To Love • American Pie • Born To Be Wild • Cold As Ice • Dust In The Wind • Free Bird • Goodbye Yellow Brick Road • Groovin' • Hey Jude • I Love Rock N Roll • Lay Down Sally • Layla • Livin' On A Prayer • Louie Louie • Maggie May • Me And Bobby McGee • Monday, Monday • Owner Of A Lonely Heart • Shout • Walk This Way • We Didn't Start The Fire • You Really Got Me • and more.
00311566..$19.95

Big Book Of Movie And TV Themes
Over 90 familiar themes, including: Alfred Hitchcock Theme • Beauty And The Beast • Candle On The Water • Theme From *E.T.* • Endless Love • Hawaii Five-O • I Love Lucy • Theme From *Jaws* • Jetsons • Major Dad Theme • The Masterpiece • Mickey Mouse March • The Munsters Theme • Theme From *Murder, She Wrote* • Mystery • Somewhere Out There • Unchained Melody • Won't You Be My Neighbor • and more!
00311582 ....$19.95

The Best Rock Songs Ever
70 of the best rock songs from yesterday and today, including: All Day And All Of The Night • All Shook Up • Ballroom Blitz • Bennie And The Jets • Blue Suede Shoes • Born To Be Wild • Boys Are Back In Town • Every Breath You Take • Faith • Free Bird • Hey Jude • I Still Haven't Found What I'm Looking For • Livin' On A Prayer • Lola • Louie Louie • Maggie May • Money • (She's) Some Kind Of Wonderful • Takin' Care Of Business • Walk This Way • We Didn't Start The Fire • We Got The Beat • Wild Thing • more!
00490424 ....$16.95

The Best Of 90s Rock
30 songs, including: Alive • I'd Do Anything For Love (But I Won't Do That) • Livin' On The Edge • Losing My Religion • Two Princes • Walking On Broken Glass • Wind Of Change • and more.
00311668 ....$14.95

35 Classic Hits
35 contemporary favorites, including: Beauty And The Beast • Dust In The Wind • Just The Way You Are • Moon River • The River Of Dreams • Somewhere Out There • Tears In Heaven • When I Fall In Love • A Whole New World (Aladdin's Theme) • and more.
00311654 ....$12.95

55 Contemporary Standards
55 favorites, including: Alfie • Beauty And The Beast • Can't Help Falling In Love • Candle In The Wind • Have I Told You Lately • How Am I Supposed To Live Without You • Memory • The River Of Dreams • Sea Of Love • Tears In Heaven • Up Where We Belong • When I Fall In Love • and more.
00311670 ....$15.95

Women of Modern Rock
25 songs from contemporary chanteuses, including: As I Lay Me Down • Connection • Feed The Tree • Galileo • Here And Now • Look What Love Has Done • Love Sneakin' Up On You • Walking On Broken Glass • You Oughta Know • Zombie • and more.
00310093 ....$14.95

Jock Rock Hits
32 stadium-shaking favorites, including: Another One Bites The Dust • The Boys Are Back In Town • Freeze-Frame • Gonna Make You Sweat (Everybody Dance Now) • I Got You (I Feel Good) • Na Na Hey Hey Kiss Him Goodbye • Rock & Roll – Part II (The Hey Song) • Shout • Tequila • We Are The Champions • We Will Rock You • Whoomp! (There It Is) • Wild Thing • and more.
00310105 ....$14.95

Rock Ballads
31 sentimental favorites, including: All For Love • Bed Of Roses • Dust In The Wind • Everybody Hurts • Right Here Waiting • Tears In Heaven • and more.
00311673 ....$14.95